CHARLESTON
HISTORY
IN COLOR

CHARLESTON
HISTORY
IN COLOR

PHOTOGRAPHS FROM THE CIVIL WAR TO MODERN DAYS

MARK R. JONES

PHOTOGRAPHS COLORIZED BY LEWIS HAYES JR.

THE
History
PRESS

Published by The History Press
Charleston, SC
www.historypress.com

First published 2023

Manufactured in the United States

ISBN 9781467154604

Library of Congress Control Number: 2023934781

Mark Jones: To my wife, Kari Jones,
always my first reader and first in everything else.

Lewis Hayes: To my father, Lewis Hayes Sr.,
the inspiration for my love of history and art.
And to my wife, Tina,
for allowing me the time to pursue my dream.

CONTENTS

1
PLANTATION LIFE AND SLAVERY

I n twenty-first-century America, the word *plantation* is mainly associated with the pre–Civil War slave labor farms, which often measured in thousands of acres. In the Lowcountry, the plantation culture was well established by 1700, fueling the extravagant lifestyle of planter families.

When Charles Town was settled in 1670, the Lords Proprietor intended to divide Carolina into twelve-thousand-acre baronies, an attempt to establish the colonial equivalent of lords and earls. Several Proprietors had a stake in the Royal Africa Company, which profited by purchasing and shipping enslaved Africans. So, from the beginning, Carolina was intended to be a slave-based colony. The first slave arrived in Charleston on August 23, 1670. During the next twenty-five years, one-quarter of the settlers were African, and it was on the institution of slavery that the great wealth of the colony was created.

Slave ships became notorious for their foul smell and high death rates due to the overcrowded, unsanitary conditions, as slaver captains attempted to maximize profits by sheer volume. The ships had poor food and insufficient drinking water, and the long voyages were rampant with epidemic diseases, which resulted in staggeringly high death rates, averaging at least 15 percent of their human cargo. Before the American Revolution, more than 40 percent of the African slaves reaching the British colonies passed through South Carolina.

In 1708, of the 9,500 people living in Carolina, 3,000 were slaves, 31 percent of the population. Sixteen years later, that number had risen to 69

Plantation washing day. *Library of Congress.*

percent. For the next 140 years, white people remained a distinct minority with little exception. The 1860 census recorded 4.4 million Africans living in America, 3.95 million of them held in bondage, including 700,000 in South Carolina, more than 57 percent of the population.

The harsh reality of creating a new colony was unsuited to an English country gentleman, so Carolina became dominated by the younger sons of West Indian aristocracy who had been tempered by the harsher life in Barbados. They embraced the idea that property was the basis of wealth

Slave Population of South Carolina 1708-1860

YEAR	NUMBER OF SLAVES	TOTAL POPULATION	% OF ENSLAVED POPULATION
1708	3,000	9,500	31.5
1724	32,000	46,000	69.5
1750	39,000	64,000	60.9
1760	57,253	76,000	75
1765	90,000	130,000	69.2
1790	107,094	249,073	42
1800	149,338	345,591	42.1
1810	196,365	415,115	46.1
1820	258,475	502,741	50.2
1830	315,401	581,185	53.9
1840	327,038	594,398	53.9
1850	384,984	668,507	57.6
1860	402,406	703,708	57.2

Slave population chart. *Created by author.*

and quickly settled on rice as their path to prosperity. For the next 150 years, rice dominated the Lowcountry economy, making Charleston one of the richest cities in the world—a wealth built primarily on slave labor.

Rice cultivation is difficult under any circumstances, but in the Lowcountry swamps, it was arduous and often lethal, due to mosquito-borne diseases, venomous snakes, alligators and brutal labor hours. The morbidity rate among white Europeans was so high that the rice industry became dominated by enslaved Black West Africans, due to their familiarity with rice culture and their greater immunity to "swamp fever."

During the heat of the summer season, planters left their plantations in the care of overseers. This facilitated the development of a more insulated slave population compared to other parts of the South. Since most of these slaves were from the same regions of Africa, they developed a culture based

Sweet potato planting, Hopkinson's Plantation. *Library of Congress.*

on common elements of language, food and other cultural touchstones, creating the Gullah community in the Lowcountry.

Most planters took for granted that slaves would die early from overwork, disease, injury, neglect or starvation. Most women spent sixteen hours daily pounding rice with mortar and pestle, while the men did the backbreaking labor in the heat of the Lowcountry marsh. After working their "sunup-to-sundown" shift on the plantation, they also had to then grow their own food and make their own clothes.

In 1699, three hundred tons of rice were exported from Charles Town. In the 1740s, that number averaged more than fourteen thousand tons and rose to more than twenty-eight thousand tons in the years before the American Revolution. In the 1840s, Carolina was responsible for 75 percent of the rice produced in North America. At the turn of the twentieth century, several hurricanes destroyed so much rice infrastructure that it had ceased to be a viable commercial activity by 1920.

In 1774, the Continental Congress pledged that "we will neither import nor purchase any slave imported after the first day of December next; after

Unloading the Rice-Barges.

Unloading rice barges. *New York Public Library.*

Rice barge and workers. *Library of Congress.*

ABOVE Charleston slave auctions. *Top*: Street auction, from a sketch by Eyre Crowe for the *Illustrated London News. Bottom*: Indoor slave auction, from *Frank Leslie's Illustrated News.*

OPPOSITE, TOP Rice fields. *Library of Congress.*

OPPOSITE, BOTTOM Charleston fish and oyster workers. *Library of Congress.*

ABOVE Picking cotton. *Library of Congress.*

OPPOSITE, TOP Advertisements for slave auctions in Charleston, 1769 and 1852. *New York Public Library.*

OPPOSITE, BOTTOM Cotton bales along the wharf, East Bay Street. *Library of Congress.*

CHARLESTOWN, *April 27, 1769.*

TO BE SOLD,

On WEDNESDAY the *Tenth Day of* MAY next,

A CHOICE CARGO OF

Two Hundred & Fifty

NEGROES:

ARRIVED in the Ship

COUNTESS of SUSSEX, THOMAS DAVIES, Master, directly from GAMBIA, by

JOHN CHAPMAN, & Co.

⁎⁎ THIS is the *Veſſel* that had the *Small-Pox* on *Board* at the *Time* of her *Arrival* the 31ſt of *March* laſt : *Every neceſſary Precaution* hath ſince been taken to *cleanſe* both *Ship* and *Cargo* thoroughly, ſo that thoſe who may be inclined to *purchaſe* need not be under the leaſt *Apprehenſion* of *Danger* from *Infection.*

The NEGROES *are allowed to be the likelieſt Parcel that have been imported this Seaſon.*

GANG OF 25 SEA ISLAND

COTTON AND RICE NEGROES,

By LOUIS D. DE SAUSSURE.

On *THURSDAY* the 25th Sept. 1852, at 11 o'clock, A.M., will be sold at RYAN'S MART, in Chalmers Street, in the City of Charleston,

A prime gang of 25 Negroes, accustomed to the culture of Sea Island Cotton and Rice.

CONDITIONS.—One-half Cash, balance by Bond, bearing interest from day of sale, payable in one and two years, to be secured by a mortgage of the negroes and approved personal security. Purchasers to pay for papers.

No.		Age.	Capacity.	No.		Age.	Capacity.
1	Aleck.	33	Carpenter.	16	Hannah.	60	Cook.
2	Mary Ann.	31	Field hand, prime.	17	Cudjoe.	22	Prime field hand.
3—5	Louisa.	10		3—18	Nancy.	20	Prime field hand, sister of Cudjoe.
4	Aaron.	20	Prime field hand.				
5	July.	24	Prime field hand.	19	Hannah.	34	Prime field hand.
6	Carolina.	5		20	James.	18	Slight defect in knee, from a broken leg.
7	Simon.	1½		21	Richard.	9	
5—8	Daphne.	infant.		22	Thomas.	6	
				5—23	John.	3	
9	Daniel.	45	Field hand, not prime.				
10	Phillis.	32	Field hand.	1—24	Squash.	40	Prime field hand.
11	Will.	9		1—25	Thomas.	26	Prime field hand.
12	Daniel.	6					
13	Margaret.	4					
14	Delia.	2					
7—15	Hannah.	2 months.					

ABOVE View of laborers preparing cotton for gins, on Alex Knox's plantation, Mount Pleasant. *Library of Congress.*

OPPOSITE, TOP Seabrook's Plantation house on Edisto Island, with Union soldiers in boat at the dock. Built in 1810 by William Seabrook, who owned several other plantations on Wadmalaw and Hilton Head Islands. In 1862, the house was used as headquarters and provost for the Union army. *Library of Congress.*

OPPOSITE, MIDDLE Slave quarters at Seabrook's Plantation. *Library of Congress.*

OPPOSITE, BOTTOM "Gwine to de field." Edisto Island. Slaves on the Hopkinson Plantation, with two boys in a cart pulled by a donkey. *Library of Congress.*

ABOVE Rockville Plantation, near Charleston. Old Bacchus fishing from a bridge near the planter's summer residence with four children gathered on the bridge. *Library of Congress.*

OPPOSITE, TOP Planter's summer residence, Charleston area. An African American boy is holding on to the horse-drawn carriage as a man boards. Two slaves are looking out the second-floor windows, while there are two white women and a young girl on the porch. *Library of Congress.*

OPPOSITE, BOTTOM William Aiken House, 48 Elizabeth Street. Constructed in 1818 by John Robinson who sold the house as rental property to William Aiken, owner of the South Carolina Railroad and Canal Company. His son William Aiken Jr. used the house as his primary Charleston residence from the 1830s onward. Aiken Jr. owned the largest rice plantation in the state, over 1,500 acres on Jehossee Island, with more than seven hundred enslaved Africans working the property. He served as governor in 1844 and in the U.S. House of Representatives in the 1850s. The Aiken family owned the house for 142 years until, in 1975, it was donated to the Charleston Museum. It is currently owned by the Historic Charleston Foundation and is considered the best-preserved antebellum house in Charleston. *Library of Congress.*

"Freedom on the plantation." A large group of African American women laborers and a male overseer processing cotton. The Robin G. Stanford Collection. *Library of Congress.*

which time we will wholly discontinue the slave trade." No new slaves legally entered Charleston until after the Revolutionary War.

At the Constitutional Convention, many northern delegates pushed to prohibit slavery. South Carolina's delegates, led by John Rutledge, argued that the southern states "would not sign the Constitution" without a clause protecting the slave trade. The compromise reached was that Congress would not interfere with the trans-Atlantic slave trade before 1808.

On December 17, 1803, after a sixteen-year hiatus, South Carolina resumed the importation of African slaves. The next four years was a gorging of epic proportions as Charleston scrambled to import as many Africans as possible before the federal government intervened, a display of exploitation unimaginable to the modern mind. The sheer numbers of Africans packed into every ship that sailed into Charleston Harbor compounded the horrors of previous voyages. During the next five years, almost forty thousand Africans entered the port of Charleston.

In 1808, the United States ended the international slave trade, but the practice of slavery continued to be legal in much of the country. Enslaved people continued to be bought and sold within the southern states, with Charleston as the center of urban domestic slave trading. More than two million slaves were sold in local, interstate and state-ordered sales. Today, 60 percent of Black Americans trace their roots back to the Lowcountry.

2

THE GREAT FIRE

Charlestonians had always lived in fear of fire sweeping across the close-built peninsular city. White citizens also lived with the apprehension of slave insurrections, which often included the deliberate use of fire as a weapon.

On the evening of December 11, 1861, a cold front bearing high winds swept from the northeast, fanning a fire near the intersection of East Bay and Hasell Streets. Most accounts attribute the fire to slaves who had started an outdoor cooking fire next to Russell's Sash and Blind factory. The wind pushed the fire into the factory, and soon the city became, as Jacob Schirmer termed it, "a Hurricane of Fire." Pressed by ferocious winds, the fire spread in speed and intensity, rushing across the peninsula diagonally in a southwest direction. By dawn it had finally burned itself out at the western edge of Tradd Street on the Ashley River, leaving a mile-long swath of destruction. It destroyed 540 acres, 575 homes and 5 churches, with property losses estimated to be $8 million ($265 million). The flames were so intense that Confederate troops fourteen miles away and Union troops six miles out to sea could see the inferno. The largest hindrance of fighting the fire was that during most of the night, it was dead low tide. The workers found it difficult to pull enough water from the harbor into the pumper engines to combat the situation.

The *Charleston Mercury* reported that by 3:00 a.m. along Meeting Street, "nothing now remains to mark where it passed, save smoldering piles of cinders and gaunt and smoking walls and chimneys." Jacob Schirmer

Approximate Path of the Great Charleston Fire
December 11-12, 1861

Map by Mark Jones, over C. Drie's "Bird's Eye View of Charleston," 1872.

claimed the fire "continued with increased fury until 12 o'clock the next day when it ceased for want of fuel."

General Robert E. Lee, serving as commander of the Department of South Carolina, Georgia and Florida, was a guest at the Mills House Hotel. As the fire raged, Lee and several of his officers stood on the roof of the Mills, looked east and noted that the fire "seemed beyond control" and was advancing so rapidly toward the hotel it might be necessary "to prepare to leave at a moment's notice." The Mills House was saved by the staff, who placed wet blankets on the roof and draped them along the north face.

View of Meeting Street, looking south toward the Circular Church, the Mills House and St. Michael's Church. Photograph by George N. Barnard (1819–1902), April 1865. The camera was set up next to the steps of the destroyed Charleston Theater, now the Meeting Street Inn (177 Meeting). The rest of the devastation along the street is the ruins of the Express Office, the Gibbes Museum and the Executive Building. The last structure visible is the scorched north side of the Mills House Hotel. In the extreme background stands St. Michael's steeple, which escaped damage.

Dominating the eastern (*left*) view of Meeting Street are the ruins of the Circular Church, with the six massive front columns. Repairs on the steeple started soon after the fire but were abandoned in August 1863. The ruined walls and steeple of the Circular Church remained standing until their destruction by the 1886 earthquake. *Library of Congress.*

OPPOSITE, TOP Ruins of the Circular Church and Institute Hall (*foreground*). Looking east toward Market Street and East Bay Street. Clearly visible in the center background are three Federal shell holes in the warehouse along Hayne Street. *Library of Congress.*

OPPOSITE, BOTTOM Ruins of the Circular Church, looking west toward Archdale Street. Visible in the background (*left*) is the steeple of St. John's Church. Featured here are four African American boys sitting around one of the church columns. *Library of Congress.*

ABOVE Interior ruins of Circular Church, looking in from the front toward the graveyard. *Library of Congress.*

The Mills House, and adjacent ruins, looking west along Queen Street. The path of the fire down Queen Street is plainly visible, but the hotel was spared due to the heroic efforts of the staff hanging wet blankets out the windows along the western face of the building. *Library of Congress.*

Another view of the fire-scarred Mills House, looking south down Meeting Street. Clearly visible to the left is the columned façade of Hibernian Hall. *Library of Congress.*

ABOVE View down Broad Street, looking east, with ruins of St. Finbar's Roman Catholic church (*left*) and St. Michael's (*right, behind lamp post*) in the distance. To the left are the ruins of postmaster Alfred Huger's mansion. *Library of Congress.*

OPPOSITE, TOP View of ruins at 91 Queen Street, looking south down Friend (now Legare) Street, with ruins of St. Finbar's and the ruins of Alfred Huger's house on Broad Street dominating the background. The double staircase led to a wood house on a raised brick foundation. On this site, the Crafts School was constructed in 1885 and is now the Crafts House Condominium parking lot. *Library of Congress.*

OPPOSITE, BOTTOM Roper Hospital (1850), 140 Queen Street, intersection of Queen and Logan Streets. The building was spared as the path of the fire skirted along the southern side. In 1863, wounded Federal soldiers were confined in the hospital. The building did not survive the 1886 quake, and twenty years later the hospital moved to its current location on Calhoun Street. *Library of Congress.*

View of the rear of St. Finbar's, looking south from the intersection of Queen and Friend (later Legare) Streets. Visible to the left are the brick ruins of St. Andrew's Hall. The shorter chimneys with the caps are from the John Rutledge House (116 Broad Street), which survived the fire. *Library of Congress.*

Fourteen houses along Queen Street were blown up to unsuccessfully create a fire block, but it did alter the path of the fire away from Roper Hospital.

Perhaps the most ironic aspect of the fire was the utter destruction of Institute Hall on Meeting Street and St. Andrews Hall on Broad Street. Almost exactly a year before the fire, South Carolina created the Confederacy by voting itself out of the Union at St. Andrews Hall, and later that evening, the Ordinance of Secession was signed at Institute Hall.

3
CONFEDERATE CHARLESTON

The secession of South Carolina was the culmination of a thirty-year slow burn of events—political, economic and cultural. Slavery became the most contentious issue in Congress, as southern politicians were desperate to maintain the equal balance of power between free and slave states.

In 1824, Congress passed the Protective Tariff Act, designed to protect American industry in the North from cheaper British goods. Other than slavery, the Tariff Act became the major conflict that divided the North and the South. The Tariff of 1828 strengthened the tariff, and its unfairness enraged South Carolina, whose main economic engine was agriculture. The state legislature formally denounced it as the "Tariff of Abominations" and published an "Exposition and Protest," secretly written by Vice President John C. Calhoun, a Carolina native. His belief that people had the power to veto any act of the federal government that violated the Constitution was the beginning of the states' rights doctrine, which grew in intensity over the next few years.

Four years later, President Andrew Jackson signed the Tariff of 1832, reducing some of the tariff rates, but it was deemed unsatisfactory by the legislature. During a hastily organized State Nullification Convention, South Carolina adopted an ordinance of nullification, which declared that the Tariffs of both 1828 and 1832 "are unauthorized by the constitution of the United States."

President Jackson disputed a state's right to nullify a federal law, and Congress passed the Force Act, which authorized the use of military force

ABOVE Looking north on Meeting Street, 1860. The portico of the Circular Church, South Carolina Institute Hall (1854) and Nicholas Fehrenbach's Teetotal Restaurant before they were all destroyed by the fire. The Circular Church, designed by Charleston native Robert Mills, was the first major domed structure in America, and the steeple was not completed until 1838. Institute Hall was the largest meeting hall in the South, seating 2,500 people. It also hosted two meetings that changed American history: the 1860 Democratic Convention and the South Carolina Secession Conference, which led to the building often being called Secession Hall. *Library of Congress.*

OPPOSITE, TOP Market Hall (1840) was constructed as the anchor of the public market. The market sheds were constructed by 1806, and a combination mason's hall and market was erected on this site, which was destroyed in 1838 by a fire. Local architect E.B. White designed the new Market Hall in the temple form with a raised portico of four brownstone Roman Doric columns. During the war, the upper room was the Confederate recruiting office, and the United Daughters of the Confederacy have maintained a museum in the space for over one hundred years. *Library of Congress.*

OPPOSITE, BOTTOM *Left*: Senator Charles Sumner (R-Massachusetts). *Right*: Representative Preston Brooks (D-South Carolina). *Library of Congress.*

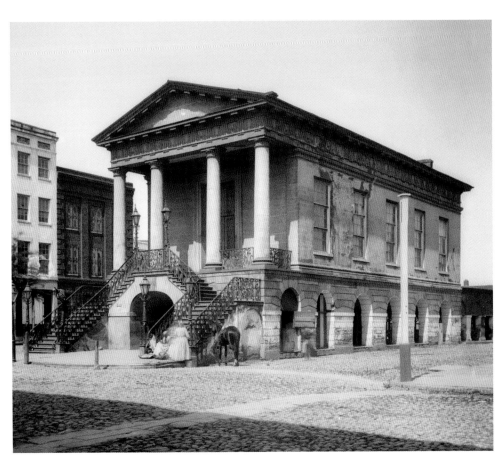

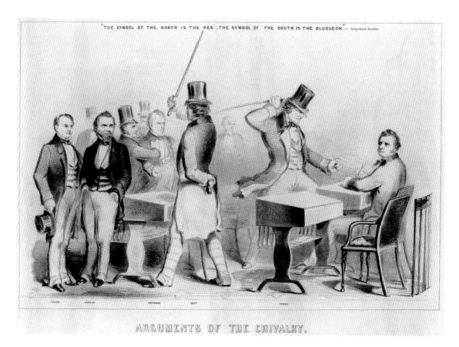

Arguments of the Chivalry, John Bufford's illustration of the beating of Charles Sumner. Brooks (*right*) is standing over Sumner (*seated*), and Representative Laurence M. Keitt (D-SC) stands (*center*) raising his cane against possible intervention while holding a pistol. In the foreground are Georgia senator Robert Toombs (*far left with hat*) and Illinois senator Stephen A. Douglas (*hands in pockets*), looking vindicated by the event. *Library of Congress.*

against any state that resisted the tariff acts. Newly elected South Carolina governor Robert Hayne raised a twenty-five-thousand-man militia to oppose the growing federal forces in the state.

Tariff policy, slavery and states' rights would continue to be national political issues for the next thirty years. In May 1856, Senator Charles Sumner of Massachusetts gave a passionate speech against slavery in which he specifically called out South Carolina senator Andrew Butler. He compared Butler's slavery support with the raping of a virgin, characterizing his affection for slavery in sexual terms.

Butler was not in attendance due to health issues, but his cousin and South Carolina representative Preston Brooks was furious and took on the duty of defending the family honor. He discussed challenging Sumner to a duel. Fellow South Carolina congressman Laurence Keitt declared that "dueling is for gentlemen of equal stature. Sumner is lower than a drunkard. Dueling with him would be an insult to yourself."

Rooftop view of Charleston from the cupola of the Charleston Orphan House (160 Calhoun Street) looking west toward the Ashley River. Visible in the left background is the West Point Rice Mill, located at 17 Lockwood Boulevard. The small, open-water pond that surrounds West Point is currently part of the City Marina along Lockwood Boulevard. *Library of Congress.*

West Point Rice Mill at 17 Lockwood Drive, built in 1840 by Jonathon Lucas and destroyed by fire in 1860. Three years later, this current structure was operational. The building is currently an events facility located in the City Marina.

Two days later, Brooks strode into the Senate chamber brandishing a cane, while Keitt held the other senators at bay. Brooks approached Sumner at his desk and said, "Mr. Sumner, I have read your speech....It is a libel on South Carolina, and Mr. Butler, who is a relative of mine." He then struck Sumner repeatedly with a cane until it broke into five pieces before several men were able to overpower Brooks.

The caning nearly killed Sumner, who became a martyr in the North, while Brooks became a hero in the South. Southerners sent Brooks hundreds of new canes in endorsement of his assault. One was inscribed, "Hit him again." As the Senate subcommittee report on the incident summarized, to most Americans it was symbolic of the "breakdown of reasoned discourse" and accelerated the country's polarization over slavery.

On July 4, 1859, Robert Barnwell Rhett, editor of the pro-secession newspaper *Charleston Mercury*, gave a speech in which he declared that "the South should either prevent the election of a Republican president in 1860, or secede."

The first non-military shot of the Civil War was fired in Charleston at the Democratic Convention of 1860. Robert W. Johannsen, in his book *Politics and the Crisis of 1860*, wrote:

> *No American political convention has ever held so much meaning for party and union....Upon the decision at Charleston rested not only the future of the Democratic Party but also the continued existence of the Union.*

Choosing Charleston as the site for the 1860 Democrat National Convention may have been an attempt to promote unity within the ranks of the party, but from the first day, the convention was in disarray. What followed was the longest and most divisive political convention in U.S. history.

After fifty-seven ballots and no presidential nominee, the convention recessed. A month later, the northern Democrats convened in Baltimore and nominated Stephen Douglas to head their ticket. The southern delegates adopted a proslavery platform and nominated Vice President John C. Breckinridge for president. The Fire-Eaters had accomplished their goal of splitting and weakening the Democrat Party, to guarantee the election of Abraham Lincoln.

On Election Day, November 6, 1860, a crowd gathered around City Hall to await the results. By midnight, there were more than four thousand people clogging Broad Street; the park behind city hall was shoulder to shoulder with citizens.

From the cupola of the Charleston Orphan House on Calhoun Street, looking east at The Citadel buildings along the edge of Marion Square. A group of people are gathered in the square. Visible in the background is the steeple of Second Presbyterian Church on Meeting Street. *Library of Congress.*

At 2:00 a.m., it was announced: Lincoln had defeated Douglas! Lincoln did not carry a single slaveholding state and won the Electoral College with less than 40 percent of the vote. A large South Carolina flag was unfurled from a window on an upper floor of the *Mercury*'s office. Robert Barnwell Rhett exclaimed, "The tea has been thrown overboard—the revolution of 1860 has been initiated."

On December 17, the secession delegates gathered in Columbia and passed a resolution that "South Carolina should forthwith secede." They also began to clamor for adjournment and moving the convention to Charleston. John A. Inglis exclaimed, "Is there any spot in South Carolina more fit for political agitation?"

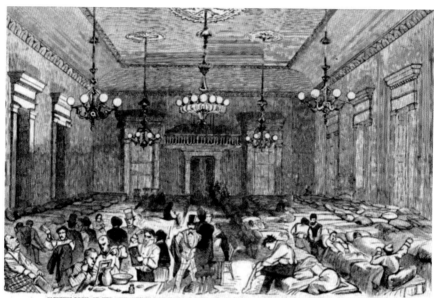

SLEEPING-ROOM OF THE NORTHWESTERN DELEGATION, HIBERNIAN HALL, CHARLESTON.—[FROM A SKETCH BY OUR OWN ARTIST.]

OPPOSITE Democratic Convention, inside Hibernian Hall and Institute Hall, from *Harper's Weekly*. *Library of Congress.*

ABOVE Vendue Range, looking west from the Cooper River docks of the Clyde Steamship Line. The French word *vendue* means "to sell," so this area was home to waterfront auctioneering businesses. The entire street sits on "made land" reclaimed from marsh in the eighteenth century. The impressive structure with the columned portico was destroyed by the 1886 earthquake and currently is the site of the Harborview Inn. The photographer is shooting from what is now Waterfront Park. *Library of Congress.*

CHARLESTON

MERCURY

EXTRA:

Passed unanimously at 1.15 o'clock, P. M. December 20th, 1860.

AN ORDINANCE

To dissolve the Union between the State of South Carolina and other States united with her under the compact entitled "The Constitution of the United States of America."

We, the People of the State of South Carolina, in Convention assembled, do declare and ordain, and it is hereby declared and ordained,

That the Ordinance adopted by us in Convention, on the twenty-third day of May, in the year of our Lord one thousand seven hundred and eighty-eight, whereby the Constitution of the United States of America was ratified, and also, all Acts and parts of Acts of the General Assembly of this State, ratifying amendments of the said Constitution, are hereby repealed; and that the union now subsisting between South Carolina and other States, under the name of "The United States of America," is hereby dissolved.

THE

UNION

IS

DISSOLVED!

Special edition "Extra" by the *Mercury*, December 20, 1860. *Library of Congress.*

Inside South Carolina Institute (Secession) Hall. From *Frank Leslie's Newspaper. Library of Congress.*

They arrived in the late morning of December 20 and entered St. Andrew's Hall. At 1:07 p.m., the roll call vote began, and every delegate voted "yea!" Forty-five days after Lincoln's election, it took eight minutes to unanimously "dissolve" the Union.

The *Mercury* had received an advance draft copy of the secession ordinance; by 1:20 p.m., five minutes after the vote concluded, the "extra" was on the streets announcing: "THE UNION IS DISSOLVED!" Tens of thousands of copies of the "extra" were printed. That night, the legislature held a celebratory signing ceremony inside a packed and raucous Institute Hall.

Meanwhile, in Charleston Harbor, the work of completing Fort Sumter progressed. Major Don Carlos Buell arrived at Fort Moultrie carrying a dispatch from the War Department ordering the garrison commander, Major Robert Anderson, "not to provoke hostilities." Anderson became fearful the garrison would soon be attacked, and by Christmas Day, the situation was so critical Anderson decided to move the garrison to Fort Sumter. That evening, the garrison began their move, and Anderson ordered the cannons

Palmetto Battery, CSA, near Charleston. George Cook, 1863. *Library of Congress.*

spiked and Moultrie set on fire. At dawn, people saw smoke rising from Fort Moultrie and quickly discovered the truth. There were no Federal troops at Moultrie—they had moved to Sumter!

Later that afternoon, from the ramparts of Fort Sumter, Anderson watched Charleston troops take possession of Castle Pinckney. Governor Andrew Pickens stopped the daily mail to and from Fort Sumter, cut off all communications and ordered the seizure of the U.S. Arsenal. By the end of the evening, South Carolina had also taken possession of Fort Moultrie and the U.S. Custom House in the Exchange Building.

Governor Andrew Pickens demanded that Fort Sumter be vacated and all Federal property in the state be surrendered to South Carolina. President Buchanan refused and threatened to order a U.S. man-of-war to Charleston but ultimately opted for the less aggressive action of chartering a civilian merchant side-wheel steamer, *Star of the West.* As the ship was known for its speed, the hope was that it would be able to slip undetected past the newly constructed Morris Island Battery. Governor

Pickens received a telegram from Secretary of the Interior Thomas, from Mississippi and a secession supporter, with the news that Washington was going to try to resupply Fort Sumter.

On the evening of January 8, 1861, the *Star of the West*, loaded with supplies and 250 new recruits, arrived at the mouth of Charleston Harbor. Being unfamiliar with the channel, and with the lighthouse and harbor lights extinguished, Captain McGowan decided to wait for dawn to make the run to Fort Sumter.

As the *Star* approached the harbor, George E. Haynesworth fired a warning shot from Morris Island across the bow of the *Star*. During the next several minutes, The Citadel cadets fired seventeen shots, with three hitting the *Star*. Captain McGowan turned his ship around and quickly left the harbor without completing the mission.

The *Charleston Mercury* of January 10, 1861, announced:

> *Yesterday will be remembered in history. The expulsion of the* Star of the West *from Charleston Harbor yesterday morning was the opening ball of the Revolution.*

Major Anderson directs the overnight move of the Federal garrison from Fort Moultrie to Fort Sumter. From *Harper's Weekly. Library of Congress.*

The taking of Castle Pinckney. From *Frank Leslie's Illustrated Newspaper. Library of Congress.*

Castle Pinckney barracks, August 1861. Located on Shute's Folly, a small island in the harbor, a log and earthen fort was built in 1797 and named after Charles Cotesworth Pinckney. During the War of 1812, a more substantial brick-and-mortar fort was constructed, renamed Castle Pinckney. On December 27, 1860, Castle Pinckney became the first U.S. military installation seized by the South. During the war, the Charleston Zouave Cadets, a light infantry unit inspired by the French forces in North Africa, garrisoned the fort. *Library of Congress.*

Pierre Gustave Toutant Beauregard was appointed brigadier general in the Provisional Army of the Confederate States. Confederate president Jefferson Davis ordered Beauregard to take command of Charleston's defenses. He seemed to be a perfect fit, an experienced military engineer and a Southern (Louisiana) gentleman.

Beauregard arrived in Charleston on March 3 and inspected the defenses of the harbor, which he found to be in disarray. On April 10, Beauregard received orders from the Confederate command in Montgomery, Alabama, that he was to open fire on Sumter "at once." The next afternoon, a boat carrying two of Beauregard's aides arrived at Fort Sumter and demanded the surrender of the fort. Major Anderson replied that he was "unable to comply" with the request to surrender.

On April 12, 1861, at 4:30 a.m., the first shot of the war was fired from Fort Johnson. During the first day, 2,500 shots were exchanged. On the morning of the second day, one-fifth of Fort Sumter was on fire, and the

Castle Pinckney and Federal prisoners, bottom of image, captured at battle of Bull Run. Charleston Zouave Cadet guards on top. *Library of Congress.*

Federals had ceased all firing, as they were dealing with the blaze. By early afternoon, Major Anderson had agreed to the terms of surrender. The next morning, Sunday, the federal garrison at Sumter were ready to leave the fort.

All told, about 1,800 Confederate shots were fired into Fort Sumter, and according to Captain Abner Doubleday, "the upper story was pretty well knocked to pieces....We had to constantly climb over heaps of debris." Charleston, and America, would never be the same.

Battery Wagner (Fort Wagner) was the main fortification on Morris Island. Built during the summer of 1862, it was a powerful earthwork that stretched across the island and was designed to keep Union forces from Cummings Point, the closest land to Fort Sumter, which protected the entrance of Charleston Harbor.

The First Battle of Fort Wagner was on July 11, 1863. Under cover of protecting naval gunfire, Federal troops were repulsed by the 1,770-man

The Federal arsenal, guarded by detachments of the Washington Light Infantry. From *Frank Leslie's Illustrated Newspaper*, December 1860. *Library of Congress.*

Citadel cadets fire on the civilian steamer *Star of the West* as it attempts to reinforce Fort Sumter. From *Harper's Weekly*. *Library of Congress.*

OPPOSITE, TOP *Left*: Major Robert Anderson, commander of the U.S. garrison at Fort Sumter. *Right*: General P.G.T. Beauregard, commander of Charleston's Confederate forces. *Library of Congress.*

OPPOSITE, BOTTOM Meeting Street, looking south at St. Michael's Church, 80 Meeting Street, 1752. It has long been one of Charleston's most recognizable landmarks. George Washington worshipped here in 1791. The chancel area boasts an original Tiffany-stained glass window modeled on Raphael's *St. Michael Slaying the Dragon*. Buried in the graveyard are two signers of the U.S. Constitution: John Rutledge and Charles Cotesworth Pinckney. During the war, the steeple was used by the Charleston Signal Corps as a watchtower, and the building received damage from several Federal artillery shells. *Library of Congress.*

ABOVE Meeting Street, looking north. This photo was taken in front of 67 Meeting Street, showing the John Poyas House (*left*) and South Carolina Society Hall (*right*). Notice that St. Michael's was not its original white color, having been painted a darker hue to make it less visible for Federal artillery. Three blocks in the distance, the scaffolding protecting the fire-damaged Circular Church steeple is visible. *Library of Congress.*

ABOVE Watching the bombardment from rooftops. From *Harper's Weekly*, May 4, 1861. *Library of Congress.*

OPPOSITE, TOP Fort Sumter, April 15, 1861. This photograph was taken moments after the raising of the first official Confederate flag, called the "Stars and Bars." *Library of Congress.*

OPPOSITE, BOTTOM Fort Sumter. Two soldiers standing on the ruins of a chimney after the 1863 bombardment. *Library of Congress.*

Confederate force; 339 Union soldiers were killed, while the Confederacy lost 12 men.

The Second Battle of Fort Wagner on July 18 is more famous, featured in the 1989 film *Glory*. Led by Colonel Robert Shaw, the 54th Massachusetts Volunteer Infantry, one of the first American military units of Black soldiers, led the assault at 7.45 p.m. The soldiers crossed 1,600 yards along the narrow spits of beach sand and marshes to approach the Confederate fortifications, successfully scaled the outer wall and entered Fort Wagner. After fierce fighting, they were forced to retreat due to heavy casualties. Of the 600 men in the 54th Massachusetts, 270 were killed (including Colonel Shaw) or captured, 149 men were injured and 52 were listed as missing in action and never accounted for.

OPPOSITE Wharves along East Bay Street. *Library of Congress.*

ABOVE Interior of Confederate Fort Moultrie on Sullivan's Island, showing ruins of sally port and wall, 1865. *Library of Congress.*

ABOVE Interior of Fort Wagner in April 1865, with a view of the gun batteries. *Library of Congress.*

OPPOSITE Colonel Robert Shaw. Born into a wealthy Massachusetts family, he enlisted as a private in the U.S. Army at the outbreak of the Civil War. He was later promoted to officer and died with his African American troops during the assault on Fort Wagner. *Library of Congress.*

TOP Tents and soldiers on the beach of Morris Island. In the distance, ironclads, including USS *New Ironsides* and five Monitor-class warships, are in action against Fort Sumter and Fort Moultrie in Charleston Harbor, September 8, 1863. *Library of Congress.*

BOTTOM Morris Island, August 1863. *Library of Congress.*

Old City Jail, 21 Magazine Street, 1802. The jail was constructed in an area designated as public lands in 1680. Originally used as a public burial ground, the site became home through the years to a city-constructed powder magazine (hence the street name), a poorhouse, a slave workhouse, a hospital and finally, the jail, which also was used as a lunatic asylum. During the war, it was a prison camp under Confederate authority. Some of the prisoners included members of the Fifty-Fourth Massachusetts who survived the assault on Battery Wagner. The jail was severely damaged by the earthquake, which collapsed the magnificent tower. *Library of Congress.*

OPPOSITE, TOP View of houses along East Battery, 1865. Resulting damage from Federal shelling during the war is quite visible at the house at 25 East Battery. The structure was abandoned after the war and replaced in 1883 by a new Victorian-style house by Charles and Eliza Drayton. To its left is the Edmonston-Alston House (21 East Battery, c. 1821). The home was purchased by Charles Alston in 1838, and the family lived in the house until 1922. Farther down the street you can see the giant Tower of the Winds columns of the front portico of 13 East Battery built by William Ravenel in 1845. The columns were destroyed during the 1886 quake and never replaced. At the end of the street is the earthen south battery. *Library of Congress.*

OPPOSITE, BOTTOM This earthen battery at East and South Battery streets is also visible in the distance in the image above. The dismantled Blakely gun was just one of dozens of these rifled cannons used around Charleston during the war. Looking west down South Battery, the live oak trees of White Point Garden are visible to the left. *Library of Congress.*

ABOVE View of Hibernian Hall, 105 Meeting Street, with damage from Federal shelling visible in the building to its right. The Hibernian Society was organized in 1801 to aid Irish immigrants, and the hall was completed in 1841. During the 1860 Democrat Convention, the Douglas delegates slept inside the hall. *Library of Congress.*

Although the assault was a tactical defeat, nationwide publicity of the valiant action of the 54th Massachusetts led to more action for Black troops and inspired recruitment that gave the U.S. Army the numerical advantage for the rest of the war.

For six weeks, Union shelling toward Fort Wagner was constant, and the Confederates abandoned the fort on September 6. Although Charleston never fell to the Union, the harbor and port were effectively closed and as Secretary of the Navy Gideon Welles reported, "the commerce of Charleston has ceased." Total casualties for the Morris Island campaign were 2,318 Federals and 1,022 Confederates.

4
RECONSTRUCTION

On February 18, 1865, Union forces entered Charleston led by the Black Fifty-Fifth Massachusetts Infantry. The white citizens were stunned and shocked by the war, by the deaths of so many Southern men and by the resulting, all-consuming poverty.

More than 40 percent of the 71,000 South Carolina soldiers died or were wounded. More significantly, 400,000 slaves in South Carolina were freed, and between March and June 1865, thousands of the formerly enslaved deserted the plantations and streamed into Charleston to celebrate their new freedom. However, due to economic conditions, they were quickly reduced to living in filthy, miserable shanties along the waterfront.

The Freedmen's Bureau was organized by the Federal government for the purpose of protecting the freedmen in their relations with white people throughout the South. Many of the bureau officials were good men, but others were just out-and-out crooks. They arrived from the North under the assumption that the newly freed and their former masters were natural enemies. They often stirred up mischief by giving "the wards of the nation" (freedmen) bad advice, preaching social inequality with the goal of arousing hatred between the races. These men, white and Black, were called "carpetbaggers," and they swarmed like locusts on the reeling South. They joined forces with white Southern opportunistic renegades called "scalawags" to form the leadership of the South Carolina Republican Party.

OPPOSITE, TOP "Marching on!" The Fifty-Fifth Massachusetts Colored Regiment enters Charleston, February 21, 1865. From *Harper's Weekly. Library of Congress.*

OPPOSITE, BOTTOM Broad Street, looking west from East Bay. The gilded oak eagle pediment (right) on 16 Broad Street was placed on the building in 1817 when it was constructed as the Second Bank of the United States. The building with the columned portico (18–22 Broad Street) was demolished to make room for the People's Building in 1910. *Library of Congress.*

ABOVE Looking east down Broad Street from Meeting. City hall (80 Broad Street) in the foreground, became a provost guardhouse after the war. Four Federal soldiers and a small boy stand in front of the building. Constructed in 1800 as a bank, it was designated city hall in 1818 and has served that purpose since. *Library of Congress.*

OPPOSITE, TOP City hall with more than a dozen Federal soldiers gathered on the steps. Federal artillery damage of the Charleston County Courthouse (*left*) is visible behind the soldier standing on the sidewalk. *Library of Congress.*

OPPOSITE, BOTTOM Freedmen's School, Edisto Island, 1865. African American children stand outside of the school building along with white Freedmen's Bureau teachers. *Library of Congress.*

ABOVE Cumberland Street, 1865, looking east from Meeting Street. Pictured here are five men standing on the iron balcony. The sign in front of the building reads "Archr. McLeish Vulcan Iron Works." *Library of Congress.*

OPPOSITE, TOP View from Mills House, looking west. A few years after the war, the damage from the 1861 fire is still visible along Queen Street. Three church steeples are visible, *left to right*: Unitarian Church, St. John's Lutheran and Grace Episcopal. *Library of Congress.*

OPPOSITE, BOTTOM Church Street, looking north at the intersection of Church and Queen Streets. St. Philip's Church dominates the center of the photograph while the French Huguenot Church (*right*) features two carriage stepping blocks on the sidewalk. To the left, the cast-iron balcony and brownstone columns of the Dock Street Theater are visible. The brown sign (*left*) hanging on the street reads "Free Kindergarten." At the corner there are two African American women chatting, one pushing a perambulator. *Library of Congress.*

ABOVE Meeting Street looking north. The magnificent Charleston Hotel, 200 Meeting Street, dominates the view. Two boys are seated at the foot of the street-level square columns. The sign above them reads: "Havana Cigars & Virginia Tobacco." Down the block (*left*), an elegantly dressed lady is exiting a carriage. *Library of Congress.*

RADICAL MEMBERS
OF THE SO. CA. LEGISLATURE.

ABOVE The sixty-four radical members of the 1868 Constitutional Convention who created the new state constitution. *Courtesy of the Smithsonian National Museum of African American History and Culture.*

OPPOSITE, TOP Charleston Hotel looking south, corner of Meeting and Pinckney Streets. *Library of Congress.*

OPPOSITE, BOTTOM Tradd Street looking east. The African American woman sits on the steps of 64 Tradd Street, watching the young girl in the pink dress. *Library of Congress.*

One of the goals of the bureau was to build up the Republican Party. It quickly organized chapters of the Union League, a secret organization that mobilized freedmen to only vote Republican. Eric Foner wrote that "by the end of 1867 it seemed that virtually every black voter in the South had enrolled in the Union League." In 1867, the *New York Times* spelled out the league's goals:

> *We want the southern people well under martial law; we want to make sure that all their Negroes have the right to vote. While they are starving, they can be managed more easily. The best way is now we have got them down, to keep them down.*

In March 1867, Congress passed the Reconstruction Acts, which set out the requirements for a southern state's readmission to the Union, which included a new state constitution written and submitted to the public for approval and ratification of the Fourteenth Amendment, which granted citizenship rights to any person born in the United States. These acts unleashed an orgy of corruption and crime in South Carolina. Some 85 percent of Black voters turned out to elect delegates to a State Constitutional Convention. Of the 124 delegates to the 1868 Constitutional Convention, 73 of them had been enslaved four years before.

The delegates gathered at the Charleston Club, and for the next six weeks, these men debated and created a remarkable document. The opening paragraph of Section 1 read, "All men are born free and equal."

Some of the provisions of the 1868 Constitution included universal male suffrage, the omission of all property qualifications for office and legalized divorce; additionally, schools and the state militia were opened to white and Black South Carolinians. It was a remarkable document bestowing voting rights and educational opportunities "without regard to race or color." However, since the document had been written predominantly by Black delegates, most white citizens refused to acknowledge it believing the purpose was, as the *Charleston Mercury* stated, to "establish negro rule." The white press called it the "Africanization of South Carolina."

During the first election under the new Constitution, 31 members of the State Senate were elected; 10 were Black. In the House, 78 out of 124 were Black. Black legislators enjoyed the majority in the South Carolina House until 1874. South Carolina also established a state militia to protect Black citizens. White men refused to join, so by the end of 1869, there were 96,000 African Americans in the militia. Within four years of the conclusion of the war, the streets and highways were being patrolled by armed Black militiamen.

Church Street, south of Tradd Street, looking north. The African American boy is standing in front of the 1720 Robert Brewton House, 71 Church Street. The impressive cast-iron balcony (*right*) still exists at 78 Church Street. Its neighbor at 76 Church has been designated a National Historic Landmark as the home in which DuBose Heyward wrote the novel *Porgy*. *Library of Congress.*

Since most white citizens refused to accept the 1868 government as legitimate, they began an unrelenting grassroots campaign against the Reconstruction regime, the so-called People's War, which included propaganda, harassment, intimidation, assault and murder. The newly elected Republican officials were helpless in the face of such determined resistance.

The Ku Klux Klan was the first major offensive by white southerners against Republican Reconstruction. From 1868 to 1871, the KKK ran rampant through the state. According to Herbert Shapiro, the Klan burned buildings and the crops of whites if "they would not vote Democratic" and "would even destroy ballots of those who voted Republican."

As Robert K. Akerman wrote in the *South Carolina Encyclopedia*, General Wade Hampton, former Confederate general, called for "an end to the extreme violence…fearing that such excesses would only invite further

Ansonborough, 31–37 Hasell Street, looking east. All these were built after the 1838 fire decimated the neighborhood. They were turned into single-family tenants by John McNellage. Traditionally, this borough was home to merchants and prosperous tradesmen. *Detroit Publishing Company photograph collection, Library of Congress.*

federal intervention in the state." Hampton's stature and influence was so great that the attacks ceased immediately. Before the war, Hampton had been one of the richest men in the South. After the war, he treated his former slaves fairly, helping them adjust to their new life of freedom. He was not against the Black race but against the powers of Washington.

Hampton claimed that it was time to "dedicate themselves to the redemption of the South." For "self-defense," rifle clubs formed in Charleston, and Hampton campaigned with the clubs, while large groups of Democrat "red shirts" roamed the state armed with pistols and shotguns.

During the 1876 gubernatorial campaign, there were 55 deaths and more than 100 injured during a dozen riots and armed confrontations. In November, Hampton claimed victory over Republican governor Daniel Chamberlain, with slightly more than an 1,100-vote margin statewide.

LEFT General Wade Hampton III. *Library of Congress.*

BELOW Democratic members leaving the South Carolina House to set up their own opposing government. From *Frank Leslie's Monthly. Courtesy of the New York Public Library.*

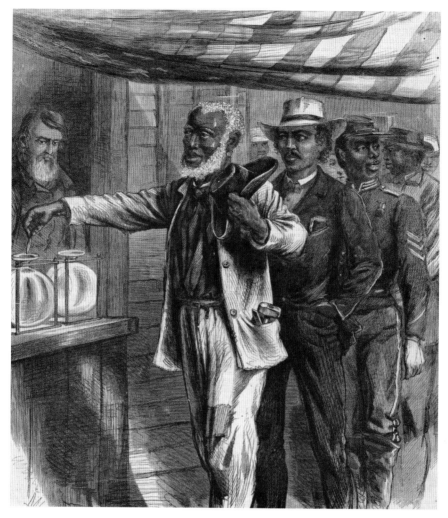

ABOVE A Black voter casting his first vote. From *Harper's Weekly*, November 17, 1867. *Library of Congress.*

OPPOSITE, TOP View from the Orphan House, looking northeast up King Street. *Library of Congress.*

OPPOSITE, BOTTOM Meeting Street, looking south at Broad Street and St. Michael's Church, 1865. City hall (*left*) appears virtually undamaged after four years of war and neglect, in comparison to the other buildings in the photo. *Library of Congress.*

OPPOSITE, TOP Meeting Street, looking north, 1910. *Right-hand side of street*: John Prioleau House (68 Meeting), South Carolina Society Hall, Judge Elihu Hall Bay House (76 Meeting) and St. Michael's Church. Dozens of pedestrians and several horse carts and automobiles are visible. *Left-hand side of street*: John Poyas House (69 Meeting) with man on bicycle. *Library of Congress.*

OPPOSITE, BOTTOM A beautiful shot of the newly rebuilt Circular Church, with St. Philip's Church visible in the background, 1890s. *Library of Congress.*

ABOVE Corner of South Battery and Meeting Street, 1870. Two African American boys are seated on a bench with three baskets at the foot of Meeting Street. In the background is 1 Meeting Street. To its left is 20 South Battery Street. *Library of Congress.*

OPPOSITE, TOP Colonial Lake, 1910. By a 1786 Act of the Assembly, the Rutledge Street Pond was turned into public lands and renamed Colonial Lake in 1881. Several of the houses in the background along Ashley Avenue were removed to make room for Sergeant Jasper Apartments and the expanded Moultrie Playground in the 1940s. *Detroit Publishing Company photograph collection, Library of Congress.*

OPPOSITE, BOTTOM South Battery and White Point Garden, along the Ashley River, 1910. *Detroit Publishing Company photograph collection, Library of Congress.*

ABOVE East Battery, looking north, 1890s. Masts of ships at Southern Wharf. *New York Public Library.*

OPPOSITE, TOP East Battery, looking north, 1906. *Detroit Publishing Company photograph collection, Library of Congress.*

OPPOSITE, BOTTOM East Battery, looking south, 1900. Twenty-five years after the war, the houses on the Battery were regaining their former opulence. *Detroit Publishing Company photograph collection, Library of Congress.*

ABOVE U.S. Custom House, 200 East Bay Street, circa 1870. Construction began in 1847 and was halted during the Civil War. It was completed in 1879. *Library of Congress.*

Democrats won 65 of 124 seats in the House, while Republicans won 59 of the 65 in the Senate. Republicans also claimed victory, citing that in two counties, the votes cast exceeded the number of voters. Governor Chamberlain ordered federal troops to the statehouse when the Republicans convened. Hampton and the Democrats set up *their* government in Carolina Hall.

Hampton requested that South Carolinians refuse to pay taxes to the Chamberlain government and asked them to contribute just 10 percent of what their tax bill had been the previous year to *his* government. South Carolinians paid taxes to the Hampton government, which denied the Chamberlain government its legitimacy. For the next four months, South Carolina had two governments and two governors. In 1877, President Rutherford B. Hayes ordered the removal of federal troops from South Carolina, which led Chamberlain and the Republican government to finally concede the election to Wade Hampton.

One aspect of the Citizen's War was to alter the voting laws in a way that made it more difficult to register to vote. In 1880, fifty-eight thousand Black men voted in South Carolina; eight years later, the number was reduced to fewer than fourteen thousand.

In 1885, Ben Tillman, a farmer in the upstate, began demanding a new state constitution. He was disillusioned by Governor Hampton, and Tillman's diatribes against Blacks, bankers and aristocrats began to attract voters. During the 1890 campaign for governor, Tillman stated, "We do not intend to submit to Negro domination and all the Yankees from Cape Cod to hell can't make us submit to it."

Tillman won the election, and a new state constitution was ratified in December 1895, which eliminated all the achievements of the 1868 Constitution. It laid out precise voting requirements, intended to disenfranchise Black men. Within a few years, registered Republicans in South Carolina dropped from twenty thousand to fewer than five thousand. Very quickly, Black voters were excluded from Democrat primaries and could vote only in the general election.

By 1896, the Black population of South Carolina numbered 728,934—60 percent of the population—but only 5,500 Black voters were registered. After the *Plessy v. Ferguson* decision ruled that racial segregation laws did not violate the U.S. Constitution, the "separate but equal" doctrine became standard across the country.

5
THE GREAT QUAKE

Tuesday night, August 31, everything in Charleston seemed normal. It had been a typically humid day, with a stifling stillness of the air that made the heat more oppressive. Many businesses and offices were closed. At dusk, due to lack of breeze, "a peculiar sulphurous odor permeated the city," as author Richard Cote described it.

At 9:51 p.m., the rumbling started and lasted nearly a minute, collapsing and damaging thousands of buildings across South Carolina. Dams broke, flooding thousands of acres of farmland. Railroad tracks buckled and trains derailed. Due to lack of granite beneath the land of the Lowcountry, the ground liquefied and water either shot out from the earth or bubbled beneath the surface of the dirt. Within fifteen minutes, most of the progress Charleston had managed postwar was undone by Mother Nature.

At 19 Broad Street, Carl McKinley, assistant editor of the *News and Courier*, was disturbed at his desk by a sound that he thought was an iron safe being rolled down the hall. McKinley later described the moment:

> The long roll deepened and spread into an awful roar....The floors were heaving underfoot, the surrounding walls and partitions visibly swayed to and from, the crash of falling masses of stone and brick and mortar filled the ears.

Seven more shocks hit the city before 8:30 a.m. Each shock sent new panic through the city as more buildings crumbled. As dawn illuminated

ABOVE Fleeing in the streets. From *The Graphic*, London, 1886. *Author's collection.*

OPPOSITE Severe damage of St. Philip's Church on Church Street, looking north toward Market Street. From *Cook's Earthquake Views. South Caroliniana Library, University of South Carolina.*

the city, locals were able to assess the magnitude of the damage. There were 124 dead, more than 200 people injured. All the hospitals were destroyed, as well as all communication connections to the outside world; telegraph poles were felled and lines snapped. Fourteen thousand brick chimneys collapsed, and hundreds of buildings crumbled, pieces of façades tumbling into the street.

The most immediate need was the housing of people, and several "tent cities" were established, using sails from ships in the harbor. Any undamaged structure with a floor and roof was turned into housing—boxcars, cargo holds of ships docked along East Bay and horse stables. More than forty thousand people slept outside for several months. In their book *Upheaval in Charleston*, Susan Millar Williams and Stephen G. Hoffius wrote:

> *Shattered were the walls that separated rich from poor, white from black....*
> *The earthquake had shifted not only the ground, but also the tenuous social*
> *structure of the city.*

Destruction along King Street near Queen Street, looking north. Pedestrians standing together along the extreme bottom left of the photo. *Library of Congress.*

News and Courier building at 19 Broad Street. Built in 1817, it became the newspaper office in 1873. *South Caroliniana Library, University of South Carolina.*

The home of lawyer B. Pressley Smith, 88 Beaufain Street, between Pitt and Smith Streets. From *Cook's Earthquake Views. South Caroliniana Library, University of South Carolina.*

Camping out in Charleston after the quake. From *The Graphic*, London, 1886. *Public domain, from the author's collection.*

TOP St. Michael's Church, sustained widespread damage from the quake. A large crack is visible running down the entire north side of the exterior wall. From *Cook's Earthquake Views. South Caroliniana Library, University of South Carolina.*

BOTTOM William Ravenel built this magnificent house at 13 East Battery in 1845. The two-story portico with Tower of the Winds columns collapsed during the quake and have never been replaced. *Library of Congress.*

View of St. John's Lutheran (1818) and the Unitarian Churches (1772) along Archdale Street. St. John's survived the quake with little damage. However, the Unitarian building sustained such significant damage that most of the exterior ornamentation of the tower was removed, and the interior was extensively restored. *Library of Congress.*

Randolph Hall was built in the 1820s as the main building on the campus of the College of Charleston. The two east and west wings of the building collapsed during the quake. Two workers (*left*) can be sitting on the ruins of the west wing. *South Caroliniana Library, University of South Carolina.*

City Hall Park, now Washington Park, looking north toward Chalmers Street. Hundreds of citizens lived in the park in tents in the aftermath of the quake. The white building in the right background is 29 Chalmers Street. Directly center in the background, the three-story brick house (38 Chalmers) was built in 1835 by Jane Wightman, the free Black daughter of Dr. William Wightman. *Library of Congress.*

Since the Richter Scale was fifty years in the future, scientists can only estimate the magnitude of the Charleston quake. Most of them agree that it would have registered at the 7.3–7.5 range, approximately in the same range as the more famous 1906 San Francisco quake. Tremors were felt from Maine to Florida and as far west as the Mississippi River, an area of approximately two million square miles. Some 76 percent of brick buildings were damaged and needed to be repaired. There were more than five hundred aftershocks over the next three years.

Carl McKinley wrote, "It seemed that God had laid His hand on in anger of His creation."

6

MODERN CHARLESTON

C harleston staggered into the twentieth century as a fully segregated city. "White Only" and "Colored" signs were posted on drinking fountains, restrooms, restaurants, hotels and parks. Black patrons were prohibited from riding the city's new electric trolly system. Thirty years after the remarkable 1868 Constitution had given them their first taste of self-determination, Black South Carolinians had been forced back into second-class citizenship.

Dr. J. Mercier Green, the city's health officer, reported that "most of the city's Afro-American population was huddled together in unfit and dilapidated structures." Many of the streets in poor neighborhoods were "little more than open sewers," which led to rampant unsanitary conditions and a high incidence of typhoid and yellow fever.

The statewide dispensary system, an attempt to clamp down on alcohol consumption, was wholly circumvented in Charleston as local bootleggers ignored the dispensary. Reverend Arthur Crain complained, "I can meet more drunken men in a fifteen-minute walk in Charleston than I could in New York, Chicago, or any other city. The city is wide open. No liquor law is being enforced."

Charleston's economy was stagnant, and city leaders were determined to bolster its fortunes in any way possible. The city sold 170 acres of land along the Cooper River for the construction of a naval shipyard. It also endorsed the plan for the South Carolina Inter-State and West Indian Exposition despite widespread skepticism. Many of the Charleston bluebloods felt

The Pink House, 17 Chalmers Street, is one of the oldest buildings in Charleston, circa 1712. Constructed partly of Bermuda stone, with a gambrel roof, it operated as a tavern during the colonial days and is one of Charleston's most recognizable landmarks. The building to its left no longer exists and is currently a parking lot. *Library of Congress.*

Title page of the Charleston Expo Official Guide. *Author's collection.*

that the fair was "unseemly self-promotion." Nevertheless, the exposition was approved, and the three main buildings were constructed on the site of the former Washington Race Course. Grouped together, they were called the "Ivory City."

More than 22,000 people attended on the first day, but the expo was not successful. For the fair's seven-month run from December 1901 to June 1902, the weather was mostly bad, there was a shortage of funds and attendance was poor—with a count of 674,000 people. Total cost was $1.2 million, and the gate receipts were just over $300,000.

Afterward, the city purchased the exposition grounds for $25,000 with the plan to build a public park on the site to be named Hampton Park, in honor of former Confederate general and governor Wade Hampton III.

The gateposts from the former Washington Race Course were donated to August Belmont, who was building the largest horse-racing facility in the country in New York, named Belmont Park. The "gift" to a Yankee millionaire was not universally popular among the people of Charleston. The idea of "Yankees" taking away Charleston relics soon became a common complaint that would later jump-start the city's preservation efforts and was trumpeted by the chamber of commerce to boost tourism.

Despite the expo's failure, the city struggled forward, and progress sometimes followed. A new hospital was constructed. The first vaudeville season opened at the Academy of Music on King Street. New sewer lines were installed in 1909. A hurricane hit in 1911, with property losses totaling more than $1 million, and two years later, there was a major program to pave most of the major streets.

World War I brought a major expansion to the Navy Yard, but there were complaints that the incidence of venereal disease was "three times higher among sailors…in Charleston" than elsewhere. In September 1918, the worldwide Spanish influenza epidemic hit Charleston, killing 450 people, with more than 18,000 citizens suffering from the illness. The next year, 90 percent of the sea island cotton crop was destroyed by the boll weevil. A local chapter of the NAACP was established by twenty-nine "Afro-Americans."

Corner of
Market and
Meeting Streets.
The "Granite
Works" red sign
would be at 120
Meeting Street.
Library of Congress.

View from Mills House, looking west, 1900. Six church steeples are visible, *from left to right*: Unitarian, St. John's Lutheran (6 and 10 Archdale Street), Grace Episcopal (100 Wentworth Street), Cathedral of St. Luke and St. Paul in the far distance (126 Coming Street), St. Patrick's Catholic (134 St. Philip's Street) and St. Matthew's German Lutheran (405 King Street). To the left of St. Matthew's, the cupola of the Charleston Orphan House is clearly visible. *Library of Congress.*

Meeting Street looking south, 1907. Dominating the photo is the Charleston Hotel (*left*) between Pinckney and Hayne Streets. In the background, St. Michael's Church is visible six blocks away. *Library of Congress.*

In January 1920, the National Prohibition Act took effect, prohibiting the production, importation, transportation and sale of alcoholic beverages. Charleston mayor Burnet Rhett Maybank clearly stated the city's position: "It does not matter whether or not the sale of alcohol is legal. Since tourists want it, and Charleston wants tourists, we will give liquor to them legal or not."

Without a doubt, Prohibition helped create the flapper, the Jazz Age, and the Roaring Twenties. Women had aggressively entered the workforce during the war and were hesitant to give up their newfound freedom. They had also recently won the right to vote and were not anxious to be forced back into their humdrum domestic roles.

In Charleston, the heightened awareness of "Yankees" taking away "relics" led a group to form the Preservation Society. The Poetry Society and the Charleston Etcher's Club were also formed in 1923, with the stated goal of "recall[ing] Charleston's past in print" and the quaint nature of Charleston's landscape through watercolors and etchings. Led by DuBose Heyward, this artistic renaissance ran parallel to the national Roaring

Flappers were the new modern women of the 1920s. *Library of Congress.*

Twenties cultural explosion. Both groups discovered that much of their creativity was inspired through the exploration of the African "Gullah" culture, which was as integral a part of Charleston's fabric as heat, rice and white aristocracy.

As Stephanie Yuhl commented, this cultural renaissance lured "high-class winter colonists" to spend several months a year in the Lowcountry. Meigs Russell, manager of the Charleston Chamber of Commerce, declared, "There is no source from which new money can be brought in here except through the medium of tourists." This ultimately led to the creation of Charleston's first historic district, which placed zoning restrictions on all historic structures in the lower part of the city. Charleston, after a long exile, was sneaking back into mainstream American culture for the crassest of reasons—money. And by 1923, the entire world had become newly aware of Charleston.

On October 29, 1923, a new Broadway show named *Runnin' Wild* debuted. The first act ends with a dance called "the Charleston." Dance historians have

Market Hall, 1900. A twentieth-century view with a mixture of wagons and automobiles, African American workers and Charleston ladies walking in front of the hall. The awning to the right is Hein's & Lesemann. *Library of Congress.*

Market Street, looking east. Turkey buzzards acted as the sanitation crew of the Market, cleaning up the disposed edible waste tossed out by the vendors. Watching their progress is a Charleston policeman and several market vendors. *Library of Congress.*

View of South Battery Street looking west between Meeting and King Streets overlooking White Point Garden. The first mansion visible on the right is 20 South Battery, constructed in 1843. In 1920, Susan Pringle Frost organized the Preservation Society of Charleston inside the house. *Detroit Publishing Company photograph collection, Library of Congress.*

commented that the branle of 1520 and the Charleston dance step of the 1920s have similar styles. They also speculate the Ashanti people of Africa were the originators of the dance step since some of their tribal dances incorporate what could be viewed as Charleston-style steps and movements. In his autobiography, jazz musician Willie "the Lion" Smith declared:

> *I say the Geechie dance had been around New York for many years....The kids from the Jenkins Orphanage Band of Charleston used to do Geechie steps when they were in New York on their yearly tour.*

It can safely be accepted that the origins of the Charleston are most likely a combination of all the above. What cannot be denied is that by the end of 1923, everybody in the country was doin' the Charleston. Nothing else epitomizes the spirit and joyous exuberance of one the most tumultuous decades in American history as the Charleston dance. Other dance crazes

St. Michael's Church looking north, with the camera placed at 69 Meeting Street. Half a dozen pedestrians are visible, as are trolley tracks, one horse and a cart in front of the church. *Library of Congress.*

Gibbes Memorial Art Gallery, 135 Meeting Street. Originally the site of the Express Office, which was destroyed by the 1861 fire. In 1904, the city received a $120,000 bequeath from James Gibbes to establish an art gallery and school. The result was this magnificent Beaux-Arts structure. *Detroit Publishing Company photograph collection, Library of Congress.*

Slave dancing on the plantation, 1820s. *Library of Congress.*

In 1926, South Carolina congressman Thomas McMillian dances "the Charleston" with Ruth Bennett and Sylvia Clairus in Washington, D.C. By this point in the Roaring Twenties, America was Charleston mad. However, many ministers preached against the evils of dancing, claiming "the road to hell is paved with jazz steps." *Library of Congress.*

By 1923, the entire world was Charleston mad. *Library of Congress.*

View from St. Michael's Church, looking north up Meeting Street. Visible in the foreground (*center*) is the four-columned Fireproof Building at Chalmers Street. Next is the Romanesque steeple of the Circular Church at 150 Meeting Street. Off in the distance (*left*) is the steeple of St. Matthew's German Lutheran Church on King Street. *Library of Congress.*

Washington Square, as seen from St. Michael's Church steeple. Clearly visible in the park is the obelisk, a memorial to Charleston's Washington Light Infantry. Visible in the distance are the steeples of the Circular Church (*left*) and St. Philip's Church (*right*). Also visible is the U.S. Custom House (*right*) on East Bay Street. *Detroit Publishing Company photograph collection, Library of Congress.*

have had their fifteen minutes of fame. None of them, however, managed to influence and infect an entire generation so thoroughly the way the Charleston did. One hundred years later, the image of the Jazz Age is always a flapper doing the Charleston. No other American decade can so neatly be summed up in one simple image.

In 1923, Thomas Porcher Stoney became the youngest mayor in Charleston history at age thirty-four. He embraced the new, modern politics by asking two women to run for city council as part of his agenda and was for "clean politics and efficient government." He served two terms, and some of his major accomplishments were the creation of a municipal airport, the Ashley River Bridge and the third-largest cantilevered bridge in the world, known as the Cooper River Bridge. In 1924, the magnificent Francis Marion Hotel opened at a cost of $1.5 million and was considered the largest and grandest hotel in the Carolinas. Soon after, South Carolina's first radio station signed on the air, WCSC-AM, broadcasting from a studio in the mezzanine from the Francis Marion Hotel.

Stoney also was an enthusiastic booster of the tourist trade and was the first to describe Charleston as "America's most historic city." Knowing that many of the elites were against tourism, he told them, "We have to sell the city… to the outside world. All we need is the right mental attitude." By the end of the 1920s, forty-seven thousand tourists visited annually. However, William Watts, speaking for many of the old families, commented, "Nothing is more dreadful than tourists.…They will make Charleston rich and ruin her."

DuBose Heyward published a novel titled *Porgy*, the story of a crippled beggar on the streets of Charleston. Two years later, the novel was adapted into a play by Heyward and his wife, Dorothy. Within a week, *Porgy* was playing to standing-room-only audiences. It closed after 367 performances and was an overwhelming success. During its run, *Porgy* employed more than sixty black performers in a serious drama, unheard of on Broadway at that time. Before the play was completed, composer George Gershwin was in discussions with Heyward to create an operatic version of the novel and play, to be called *Porgy and Bess*.

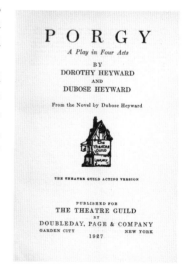

Cover of script for the *Porgy* Broadway production. *Author's collection.*

Charleston Orphan House, 1794, at the corner of Calhoun and St. Philip's Streets, America's first public orphan house. When constructed, it was the largest building in Charleston and served its purpose for the next 150 years. It was demolished in 1956 to make room for a Sears-Roebuck store and is currently the location of the College of Charleston's Joseph E. Berry Dormitory. *Library of Congress.*

Cathedral of St. John the Baptist, 122 Broad Street, 1907. The site was purchased by Bishop John England in 1821. Thirty years later, the first cathedral was built, but destroyed in the 1861 fire. Between 1890 and 1907, the debris from the ruined cathedral was removed and the new Gothic Revival structure was completed in 1907. Due to lack of funds, the one-hundred-foot spire in the original plans was not completed until 2010. *Detroit Publishing Company photograph collection, Library of Congress, 1907.*

OPPOSITE, TOP King Street, looking south, 1910. Intriguing view of Charleston's main commercial street with well-dressed pedestrians, a car, a bicyclist and several horses and carts. On the right is the Siegling Music House (243 King Street, corner of King and Beaufain Streets), which opened in 1819 and was operated by the family until 1970. *Library of Congress.*

OPPOSITE, BOTTOM King Street (corner of Hasell and King Streets) looking north, 1910. Another exciting view of Charleston's business district, filled with various automobiles, bicycles and pedestrians. The magnificent dome of the Hirsch-Israel Co. (*left*) was home to the Peoples First National Bank (275–77 King). In the far distance (*left*) is the steeple of St. Matthews German Lutheran Church. *Library of Congress.*

ABOVE Broad Street looking west from East Bay, 1920s. *Left-hand side in the shade*, the first sign reads: "Carolina Portland Cement Co. Building Material." The second sign reads: "Walker-Evans & Cogswell, Co. Stationery and Printing."
Right-hand side of the street: A cigar Indian stands on the red pedestal next to the utility pole. The green sign above reads: "Virginia-Carolina Chemical Co. Sales Department. So.Ca. Division." The red sign over the awing reads: "Follie Bros. Company. Cigars." The next red sign reads: "Henry Lewis. Drugs. Soda." The red pyramid shaped box on the curb reads: "Soda Water. Cigars. Souvenirs. Post Cards." The yellow brick eight-story People's Building looms in background. *Library of Congress.*

Administration building, Charleston Navy (Naval) Yard, Charleston, SC. *Detroit Publishing Company photograph collection, Library of Congress.*

On October 10, 1935, *Porgy and Bess* opened in New York and ran for 124 performances. Brooks Atkinson wrote in the *New York Times*, "Let it be said at once that Mr. Gershwin has contributed something glorious." Most critics were confused about the form of the show—was it an opera, or was it a musical? Gershwin himself stated, "I have created a new form, which combines opera with theater."

Charleston wasted little time taking advantage of *Porgy and Bess* for profit. It was a boon for tourism marketing, and with the Great Depression gripping America, Charleston was in no financial position to deny any windfall. DuBose Heyward's former neighborhood, where the opera takes place—Church and Tradd Streets—became a haven for tourist shops, catering to the much-disdained but much-needed Yankee trade. Several of Charleston's "first families" opened coffeehouses and tea shops, and "lady guides" conducted walking tours down cobblestone streets and brick alleys.

The theme of these tours was what the city was trying to preserve and sell—
what Rhett Butler describes in *Gone with the Wind*, "the calm dignity life can
have when it's lived by gentle folks, the genial grace of days that are gone."
The *Chicago Tribune* wrote:

> *In a world of change, Charleston changes less than anything…Serene and
> aloof…it remains a wistful reminder of a civilization that elsewhere has
> vanished from earth.*

BIBLIOGRAPHY

Articles and Papers

Jervey, Theodore D. "Charleston during the Civil War." In *Annual Report of the American Historical Association for the Year 1913*, vol. 1, 1–20. Washington, D.C.: Government Printing Office, 1915.

Shapiro, Herbert. "The Ku Klux Klan During Reconstruction: The South Carolina Episode." *Journal of Negro History* 49, no. 1 (1964): 34–55.

Books

Carney, Judith A. *Black Rice: The African Origins of Rice Cultivation in the Americas.* Cambridge, MA: Harvard University Press, 2001.

Cauthen, Charles Edward. *South Carolina Goes to War.* Columbia: University of South Carolina Press, 2005.

Channing, Steven A. *Crisis of Fear: Secession in South Carolina.* New York: Simon and Schuster, 1970.

Chibbaro, Anthony. *The Charleston Exposition.* Charleston, SC: Arcadia Press, 2001.

Cote, Richard. *City of Heroes: The Great Charleston Earthquake of 1886.* Charleston, SC: Corinthian Books, 2006.

Crooks, Daniel J., Jr. *Charleston Is Burning: Two Centuries of Fire and Flames.* Charleston, SC: The History Press, 2009.

Edgar, Walter. *South Carolina: A History.* Columbia: University of South Carolina Press, 1998.

———, ed. *The South Carolina Encyclopedia.* Columbia: University of South Carolina Press, 2006.

Emilio, Luis F. *A Brave Black Regiment: History of the Fifty-Fourth Regiment of Massachusetts Volunteer Infantry 1863–1865.* New York: Arno, 1969.

Fant, Jennie Holton, ed. *The Travelers' Charleston: Accounts of Charleston and Lowcountry, South Carolina.* Columbia: University of South Carolina Press, 2016.

Fraser, Walter J. *Charleston! Charleston! The History of a Southern City.* Columbia: University of South Carolina Press, 1989.

Gillmore, Quincy Adams. *Engineer and Artillery Operations Against the Defences of Charleston Harbor in 1863.* New York: Nostrand, 1865.

Gray, Lewis C. *History of Agriculture in the Southern United States to 1860.* 2 vols. Washington, D.C.: Carnegie Institution, 1933.

Hutchinsson, James M., and Harlan Greene. *Renaissance in Charleston.* Athens: University of Georgia Press, 2003.

Jones, Mark R. *Charleston Almanac: From Founding Through the Revolution.* Charleston, SC: East Atlantic Publishing, 2017.

Littlefield, Daniel C. *Rice and Slaves: Ethnicity and the Slave Trade in Colonial South Carolina.* Baton Rouge: Louisiana State University Press, 1981.

Marszalek, John F., ed. *The Diary of Miss Emma Holmes.* Baton Rouge: Louisiana State University Press, 1979.

Olwell, Robert. *Masters, Slaves, and Subjects: The Culture of Power in the South Carolina Low Country, 1740–1790.* Ithaca, NY: Cornell University Press, 1998.

Potter, David M. *The Impending Crisis: America Before the Civil War, 1848–1861.* New York: HarperCollins, 1976.

Powers, Bernard, E., Jr. *Black Charlestonians: A Social History, 1822–1885.* Fayetteville: University of Arkansas Press, 1994.

Roper, L.H. *Conceiving Carolina: Proprietors, Planters, and Plots, 1662–1729.* New York: Palgrave Macmillan, 2004.

Rosen, Robert. *Confederate Charleston.* Columbia: University of South Carolina Press, 1992.

———. *A Short History of Charleston.* Columbia: University of South Carolina Press, 1992.

Thomson, Jack. *Charleston at War: The Photographic Record, 1860–1865.* Gettysburg, PA: Thomas Publications, 2000.

Varon, Elizabeth R. *Disunion! The Coming of the American Civil War, 1789–1859.* Chapel Hill: University of North Carolina Press, 2008.

Wallace, David Duncan. *South Carolina: A Short History.* Columbia: University of South Carolina Press, 1951.

Wise, Stephen R. *Gate of Hell: Campaign for Charleston Harbor, 1863.* Columbia: University of South Carolina Press, 1994.

Wood, Peter H. *Black Majority: Negroes in Colonial South Carolina from 1670 Through the Stono Rebellion.* New York: Knopf, 1974.

Yuhl, Stephanie E. *A Golden Haze of Memory: The Making of Historic Charleston.* Chapel Hill: University of North Carolina Press, 2005.

Online Sources

Butler, Nic, PhD. "The End of the Trans-Atlantic Slave Trade." *Charleston Time Machine,* January 26, 2018. ccpl.org.

———. "The Rise of Voter Suppression in South Carolina, 1865–1896." *Charleston Time Machine,* October 23, 2020. www.ccpl.org.

———. "The South Carolina Constitutional Convention of 1868." *Charleston Time Machine,* March 2, 2018. www.ccpl.org.

———. "Street Auctions and Slave Marts in Antebellum Charleston." *Charleston Time Machine,* January 22, 2021. www.ccpl.org.

South Carolina Historical Society. Haas & Peale Photograph Collection, 1863. https://schistory.org.

INDEX

ABOUT THE AUTHORS

LEWIS HAYES is an Air Force veteran of the first Persian Gulf War and retired fire chief from the Croft Fire Department in Spartanburg, South Carolina. His ancestor served with George Washington and moved to South Carolina in the 1780s. Hayes's passion for history led him to colorizing black-and-white images to illuminate the past.

MARK R. JONES is a twenty-year veteran Charleston tour guide and author of eight volumes about South Carolina history, including the *Wicked Charleston* books. He has conducted more than thirty thousand tours and can be found daily on the Charleston streets. His other writings, including his "Today in Charleston History" essays, can be found at Mark-Jones-Books.com.

Visit us at
www.historypress.com
....